Change Your Life

By using the most powerful
Crystal on earth

Robert W Wood D.Hp
(Diploma in Hypnotherapy)

Rosewood Publishing

First published in U.K. 2003
By Rosewood Publishing
P.O. Box 219, Huddersfield,
West Yorkshire HD2 2YT

www.rosewood-gifts.co.uk

Copy-editing
Margaret Wakefield BA (Hons) London
www.euroreportage.co.uk

Cover photograph by
Robert W Wood D.Hp
Annabel my granddaughter

Cover and layout re-designed by
AJ Typesetting
www.ajtype.co.uk

Printed in Great Britain by
Delta Design & Print Ltd
www.deltaleeds.co.uk

ISBN 978-0-9567913-1-3   BK12

Discovering the most powerful Crystal on earth.

In the world of minerals, the most amazing and most powerful crystal of them all has got to be the Quartz family of crystals. You can find them in quartz watches and at the heart of all computers. They are even used to make the windows and the heat shields for the space shuttles, to enable astronauts to survive the intense heat from re-entry into the earth's atmosphere. The material used for this is called 'fused quartz'. Fused quartz is resistant to heat - very useful if you want to see into hot places. Another example of its use is in windows for furnaces.

The most common element on earth is oxygen, and the second is silicon. The most common of all crystals is silicon quartz, a crystal that grows from the combination of silicon and oxygen. Your computer, either at home or at work, will have in it a 'computer chip' - and it really is a 'chip'; a chip of silicon quartz crystal. That's why they call the home of computer chips, in Los Angeles, 'Silicon Valley'.

The point is that, although you may not have realised it, you are using crystals every day of the week. These crystals, in the form of computer chips, liquid crystal displays, clocking devices, etc, are extensively being used throughout the whole of the telecommunications industry, and are all doing some very important basic things with energy.

They are helping to change, maintain and manipulate the characteristics of energy, so as to perform specific tasks. They can store, amplify, correct and control energy waves.

Not so mysteriously either as it turns out, because it's a natural property of crystals to be able to do all of this. And the emphasis here is on 'natural'.

I can hear you saying: 'So how does knowing all this enable us to change our lives?' Well, it doesn't - not in itself, that is; but what you are about to discover is that 'it takes two to tango'. Have you ever used an epoxy resin glue? One company advertises that it sets super-strong in minutes and is strong enough to lift a car. The glue comes in two tubes. One's the epoxy and the other the hardener. Neither of them in themselves can do that much, but once the two are mixed together then - wow! This stuff is powerful, and it's all been done naturally by a chemical reaction. Once the two have been mixed together there is no going back. The glue has got to set.

The greatest Crystal of them all

Both carbon and silicon enjoy a special status within chemistry: carbon as an element in organic compounds, and silicon (together with oxygen) as the most important rock-forming element - rock crystal. Silicon is one of the trace elements found in the human body. Trace elements are to be understood as metals, and elements similar to metals, which occur naturally in the body in very tiny concentrations. Most of them are vitally important for man - and here we have a physical connection with crystals.

If quartz crystal is the most powerful crystal in the mineral world, then the greatest of them all in the animal kingdom, with all its multiple-combinations of trace elements, has got to be MAN.

Power, without knowledge, is useless.

Do you remember how, in the movie 'Superman', Clark Kent had all the power but not the knowledge? In the early part of the film we see him kicking a football into outer space, and racing a train and winning. His earthly father tells him, 'You are here for a reason.' However, this doesn't help Clark Kent to understand why he is different. But when he turns eighteen he takes a green crystal that was sent along as a teaching aid by his real father, Jor-El, and we see him intuitively travel to the frozen north, where he throws the green crystal and sees a crystalline building rise up from the glaciers.

Upon entering the building, Clark finds the green crystal again, and when he places it in the appropriate place on a crystalline control panel, a vision of Jor-El appears and starts to teach him who he is, what he is, where he has come from and why; all about Kryptonian, his home planet, and Kryptonian philosophy. Acquiring all this knowledge takes Clark twelve years, and we next see him no longer an eighteen-year-old boy, but a thirty-year-old man, with all the confidence and knowledge of who he is. We see an amazingly powerful, confident yet graceful figure take off and fly, and so the real story begins.

By changing the way we think, we can change the future.

It's one thing being told what we can do; but it's another understanding how to do it. Haven't we been told by religious leaders, for thousands of years, to pray? Now if we could understand the power behind the prayer, I am sure more of us would be praying. There are several natural laws of the Universe. These natural laws are exact laws that do not change; they govern all physical and mental sciences. One is the law of cause and effect, and another the law of right thinking. Right thinking starts by recognising the powers of the subconscious mind, the creative power of our thoughts and mental imaginings from within, and how it all works.

You can wish, hope, pray and worry yourself sick until you are a hundred years old. However, if you don't understand the law of right thinking (praying) by using visualisations and **'imagining with feeling'**, you will always be like a ship at sea without stabilisers, just bobbing along, being knocked from pillar to post, having to take life as it comes, believing that nothing you can do can change it. Does this sound anything like your life so far? Wouldn't you prefer to be the ship with the stabilisers? Remember it's the same seas that everybody's travelling on, with calm periods and stormy seasons. This we may not be able to change, but the way we travel, I believe we can. If given the choice, wouldn't you prefer to travel first class and with stabilisers? This book is all about discovering how you can. Take your time, because it takes time.

A journey begins.

In the study of hypnotherapy, you would probably think, like I did, that the hardest part of the course would be 'how to hypnotise someone'. So imagine my surprise to be told that it was both the simplest and the easiest part of the whole course; that the hardest was going to be the understanding beyond the teaching. A little like the difference between knowing how to drive a car and knowing how it's been designed and built. My intention here, within these writings, is to simply help direct you towards your own understanding of universal law and the law of right thinking.

What's in a number?

How many stars are there? In the Bible it says the stars are as numerous and as countless as the grains of sand on the seashore. However, science has estimated the number to be 10 to the power 21, that is 1 with 21 noughts - and this is what it looks like: 1,000,000,000,000,000,000,000. It's a lot. However, if you take the number of neurones in the brain (these are cells specialised to conduct nerve impulses) you may be surprised to find that there are 10 to the power of 12, that is 12 noughts - look: 1,000,000,000,000. But did you know Albert Einstein said that imagination was more important than knowledge? Here's an example. Who came up with the number 32,768? Was it knowledge or imagination? Scientists discovered that the atoms within a micro-thin slice of synthetic quartz crystal emit a very precise electronic pulse, when power - often from a tiny battery - is passed through it; in fact it vibrates at precisely 32,768 times per second. Now that's knowledge; but let's see what imagination did with this knowledge. Imagination discovered that if you channel the pulses through microchip circuitry, and then successively halve the pulse in a series of 15 steps, then the result is really astounding: it produces a single, constant pulse per second. This is very precise, it's even precise to within a second or two a year, which is why watches and clocks are now so accurate - a uniting of science and the imagination.

The marvel of science

Hundreds of years ago, everyone believed that the Earth was at the centre of the universe. Today we know better, but a complete picture remains elusive. From the ancient notion of a flat Earth to today's theories on the very shape of past and future history, ideas of the universe have evolved with the help of scientific discovery and the eternal human imagination. Plato spoke metaphorically of how male and female are actually the divided halves of one primordial being. Each half, Plato tells us, is looking to the other for its completeness. If we are going to take advantage of our hidden potential, that 'something' we are searching for, it may be useful to understand that the masculine and feminine sides of our psyche must be united. This theme of being united occurs regularly. It's the 'bringing together of two parts' that often holds the key, including man and crystals.

De-mystifying the mysteries.

Just because you can't see it, doesn't mean it's not there. The power behind birthstones, lucky talismans, charms, amulets and healing crystals is real: be in no doubt. We are talking POWER here, real power. For many years I have given talks entitled 'Discover the Hidden Power in Gemstones' or 'An Evening of Mystery and Imagination'. These talks on birthstones, talismans and healing crystals often include a demonstration on crystal healing, and this has nearly always produced amazing results. Over the years I have spoken to more than a thousand groups, well over one hundred thousand people in all, and I have seen and heard many unusual things.

About half my audiences are church groups, and if I have a gift at all it's being able to take 'church language' and change it into 'new age'. I try to de-mystify the mysteries, explain what may be happening and how, whilst trying to be non-judgmental. On page 18 you'll see a list of my books, written on the many subjects of birthstones, talismans and healing crystals. Within my talks there comes a point where I say, 'Either the stones work for you, or they don't.' If you win at bingo regularly and you are using a lucky bingo stone (a talisman), then you're more likely to believe in them. It's the same with healing crystals: if they have worked for you, then you'll believe.

However, according to holistic healers, when we are ill we are 'out of balance' with nature, and a crystal can help us to return back 'into balance', to good health. It's a little like when a radio station goes off station; we tune it back in, back 'into balance'. If we take the view that all this is somehow God-given, that it's the law of the universal life force and is found within the mind, then I believe within these writings you can become so empowered by discovering for yourself a code that will enable you to change your life, and that includes your health, luck and even the future.

Beginning the search.

Each one of us is responsible for our own search, a search for meaning and the choices we make, but it's worth remembering that seeking and enquiring can only have one purpose: that is, to find; and once we have found, then this stage of the journey, the search, is completed.

"There are many gates into the garden of heaven", the Sufi masters say, "but to enter the garden you need only pass through one."

The challenge is to find the right one and the right guidance. It's not easy in a world where religion can easily be transformed into inquisition, and the urge to save souls into holy wars. A way is wrong when it can harm, deceive or mislead you. All journeys start at the beginning. The fact that you are reading this book shows your intention to discover more, and the best way will be to discover for yourself those parts within us that are able to connect with the Supreme Principles of the universe. Within every human psyche there exist higher mental and emotional centres capable of unimaginable states of awareness, unless they are awakened by proper guidance, then it's likened to living your life out in the basement of a thousand roomed palace.

Mind over matter?

Can you ride a bike, or use a typewriter? Can you swim or drive a car? If the answer to any of these questions is 'yes', then you have already experienced your greatest asset from within your mind. Let me explain: there are two main parts to our brains, the conscious and subconscious. The conscious acts like a gatekeeper for the mind and has the power to direct - it's how we think; but it's the subconscious that performs the tasks. Like driving a car - you decide where you're going consciously, but it's the subconscious that does all the driving. It's as if within any skill there's a kind of 'knowing', and life becomes much more comfortable when that 'knowing' kicks in.

There are pictures that can show this effect quite clearly - for example, this shifting staircase. When you first look, you may see the staircase as if you were standing at the bottom right hand corner of the picture, ready to walk up the steps. Then it will change, almost as if by magic, so that you are now in the bottom left hand corner, underneath the steps - or vice versa.

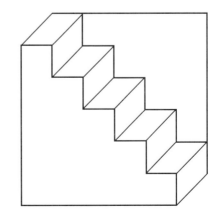

This picture is a way of revealing the subconscious, because there are two ways you can see this picture. Consciously you see it one way, but within a few seconds your subconscious sees another way of interpreting it and has to show the alternative to you, and then the picture will start to fluctuate backwards and forwards.

Think of the mind like Concorde, the supersonic plane. The pilot represents the conscious, while the subconscious is represented by the plane, the engineers who built it, the scientists that helped, the aviation authorities that allow it to fly, the ground crews including air traffic control that support it. The responsibility is with the captain - but just imagine the size of the support team. Wow! It's colossal. With the power we have within us, is it possible that minds can move matter? The answer is yes! It really can. Read my book 'Discover Why Crystal Healing Works', where I explain how I moved a mountain; or read my book on crystal dowsing. For a more everyday example, think of stomach ulcers. It's a fact that these are brought about because of the way we think, mainly due to stress and anxiety. The surgeon can repair the ulcer, but not the cause that created it.

The power of the mind.
One of the most amazing stories I ever heard was about a very wealthy woman, in her late fifties, who went for hypnotherapy. During the preliminary interview she was asked if she had ever had children. Her reply was that sadly her only regret in life was that she never had, although she had spent most of her life 'leaving no stone unturned', including consulting one of the best and most expensive gynaecologists in Harley Street.

This story I know will be difficult to believe, but it is true. During her consultations it became apparent that she had in fact in her late teens been pregnant and had had a miscarriage very late on into the pregnancy. I won't go into the details here, but the experience had been so devastatingly traumatic that her mind, the conscious mind, decided to conceal the memory from her. This can often happen after a bad car accident. Can you imagine the woman's surprise, the shock and horror when her memory decided to reveal this amazing truth about her past? It's really very rare to find such an extreme case, but this story goes on to provide an even more amazing revelation of the power within the mind. Before I tell you more I think it best if I explain a little about the power of hypnotherapy.

Hypnotherapy.
It seems to have started with 'The Psychology of the Unconscious', published in 1911 by the Swiss psychiatrist Carl Jung (1875-1961). Jung (pronounced 'Young') was the leading collaborator of Sigmund Freud (1856-1939). Jung's research into psychoanalysis led him to disagree with Freud's interpretations.

Sigmund Freud, the founder of modern psychology, discovered in 1895 that he was able to cure a patient of hysteria. Her illness was characterised by emotional outbursts and some physical symptoms, and Freud cured her by allowing her to talk freely whilst under hypnosis. Later, finding hypnosis inadequate, Freud encouraged patients just to ramble on with their thoughts; whilst in a state of relaxed consciousness. This method of drawing memories from the subconscious to the conscious mind became known as 'psychoanalysis'.

A huge difference between psychotherapy and hypnotherapy is down to timescale. Whereas psychotherapy, psychoanalysis or counselling may take one hundred hours to complete, in hypnotherapy it can take less than ten. Hypnosis speeds up the process. This type of hypnosis is certainly not like that induced by a stage hypnotist; it's more of a state of relaxed consciousness. The patient is always consciously awake.

The last resort.
Who would see a hypnotherapist? Just about anybody who has found the medical profession unable to find anything wrong, implying that their illness is psychosomatic - it's probably all in the mind. What you are discovering is just how powerful the mind is. People know when there's something wrong. Some describe it as a 'gut feeling'. Things are just not right.

Here's a rule of thumb: if everybody says, 'You're fine; you look OK; pull yourself together, there's nothing wrong,' and you know deep down that there is, then see a hypnotherapist. If you are suffering from anything that could be described as an irrational fear or phobia - for example, being scared of wasps, bees, blood, closed-in places or open spaces, or if you dare not fly but would like to - then see a hypnotherapist. They can really help. However, if everybody is telling you that there's something wrong with you and you don't think there is, then see a psychiatrist - you're probably ill.

Back to Freud.
The disagreement between Freud and Carl Jung stemmed from Freud's method of 'letting sleeping dogs lie' - in other words, what's in the past should be left in the past. Jung thought that this was the cause of all the problems later on in life. He believed that if the 'suppressed memories', as he called them, were drawn from the subconscious and brought into the conscious, the adult would be able to handle them. And the amazing thing is, he was right; once the thought or memory has been brought into the adult's conscious world, all the irrational fears and phobias just disappear for ever. The process is described by many as being 'let out of prison', 'feeling free', or 'like having a bad tooth pulled out' - it's such a relief.

The power of mind over matter.

To go back to our story of the woman who had had a miscarriage: her hypnotherapy sessions were drawn to a very successful conclusion, all repressed memories were found - a very satisfactory result. About a year later she wrote to say that she had seen her gynaecologist and had been given some surprising news. She explained that she had been unable to have children because she had had a retroverted womb (her uterus was turned backwards); but she had now been told that for some inexplicable reason it had just righted itself and was now normal. Can you see a connection? If something like a suppressed memory can have such a devastating effect as to tilt her womb, what could you do, knowing how it all works. There are thousands of such stories of 'miracles'; they're happening all around us all the time.

**Failure and success are not accidents or incidents,
they are influenced by a state of mind.**

Psychic energy.

Where do you get your energy from: introversion or extroversion? To give you an idea: imagine two friends who both teach in a school. After a full day's work one of them regularly goes and plays badminton whilst the other just wants to get home and spend a little time on their own. Now if you were the one going home tired, then you could be forgiven for thinking that there was something wrong with you, especially when your friend seems to have so much energy.

There are only two ways of acquiring psychic energy: you create it either from within - called 'introversion' - or from without - 'extroversion'. The extrovert, after a full day at school, has overcharged their batteries and needs to discharge, whilst the introvert needs to re-energise within themselves. In other words, the extrovert is drawing energy from the people around them, and the introvert is having their energy taken away from them, hence the expression 'feeling drained'. If you locked up an extrovert into solitary confinement it would probably kill them, whereas the introvert would love it. These are two extremes, but you may recognise yourself from the descriptions.

The collective unconscious.

According to Jung, the personal subconscious contains lost memories, painful ideas that are repressed. But he also identified what he called a 'collective unconscious', an extension of the personal subconscious. He believed that at this level of mind family, social groups, nations and even all humanity were connected. Imagine what he is saying: that each one of us has access to a collective subconscious. Just like the Internet, we can, through our minds, somehow connect to all of humanity. We can ask for help and know that the thought is being picked up on. As owners of our minds, our job is to make sure we are being heard. Discovering this code is mind-blowing.

You only have to ask.

It takes no more effort to aim high in life, to demand your share of good fortune, to be healthy, to have peace of mind, than it does to accept misery, ill health and poverty. Through these lines a poet correctly touched this universal truth:

> I bargained with life for a penny
> and life would pay no more,
> however I begged at evening
> when I counted my scanty store.
>
> For life is a just employer,
> he gives you what you ask;
> but once you have set the wages,
> why, you must bear the task.
>
> I worked for a menial's hire,
> only to learn, dismayed,
> that any wage I had asked of life
> life would have willingly paid.

A motivational book.

I read these words one afternoon whilst in Wales on a business trip. I don't know why, but for some reason someone staying in the same hotel the previous night had giving me a book by Napoleon Hill called 'Think and Grow Rich', a classic motivational book sharing a philosophy for achievement. I can highly recommend the book. I had some time to spare and so I read it, and the words that day seemed to be speaking to me. One of the principles was that everybody has an edge. It may be only a little thing but nevertheless we all have this edge, and the writer seemed to be saying that if we use our minds we can turn our dreams into reality - by using the right way of thinking.

It seemed to make sense, and so I tried it. You'll have to read my book 'Discover Why Crystal Healing Works" for more details, but looking back I can't believe the changes in my life. Not all were good, but it's strange how even the not-so-good have turned out for the better. I moved from a three-bedroomed semi into a four-bedroomed detached; from a salesman to a managing director, from driving an old Astra to a new Volvo 740 with built-in car phone.

A chance of a new life now awaits you. You only have to reach out and take it. But remember that it's you yourself who must do the reaching.

One of the greatest gifts on earth can be found within the mind. Once we are seriously involved in researching this, it's best to be prepared and well versed in the rules. It's the Law of Right Thinking.

Can any good come from a lie?
The answer is 'yes, if the intention is well meant'. We live our lives in the conscious world but carry with us a support pack like nothing else on earth. How it's been designed, or evolved, still remains a mystery - but not the fact that we have it. The conscious is likened to an iceberg: you can only see the tip of it, nine-tenths is below the water level. And it's the same with the mind: the bulk of it you can't see, but you can easily experience it.

Have you ever seen a stage hypnotist when he gets people to do strange and outrageous things? If you think you could never do these things, think again - because we all do, in our dreams. This is why the mind can be dangerous. If you want to know how dangerous, imagine a child running the world from a computer console. That's your subconscious; and that's why the conscious has got to be in charge.

The placebo effect.
Do you know what a placebo is? It's an inactive substance, like a sugar pill, given to a patient who insists on receiving medication, or when someone, maybe a doctor or psychologist, believes that a patient would benefit from the psychological deception of believing they have been given medication. It really is well known in the medical profession.

However, here is an amazing fact. Although it's based on a lie - someone being told that the 'medicine' they are taking will cure them - the surprise is that it actually does. How can it? And the answer is, we don't fully know. Just like we don't know what electricity is - but that doesn't stop us using it. Early man didn't know what a magnet was, but that didn't stop him circumnavigating the world using it. Today we call it a compass.

It's thought that for some, the belief that the placebo will work is enough to trigger something within the mind that reacts with the body to bring about a positive result. These are not isolated cases, in fact they are so common that whenever they are testing new drugs they do what are called 'blind clinical tests', whereby half the patients are given the proper medicine and the others the placebo. It's an attempt to show how effective the drugs really are. What would you do if you knew how this worked, and that you could use this placebo effect to your advantage!

How to change the future.

Change the way you think and you can change your future. Science may be able now to give an explanation of how all this may work. We are standing at the very edge of a staggering, unimaginable advance in science and technology. Science for the very first time can see into a whole new dimension of reality with the discovery of 'SCALAR' electromagnetic wave technology. It is through this branch of science that we will be able to cast more light on the potential capabilities of minerals, gems and crystals and their interaction with man.

Imagine you have a powerful hand-held magnet. As you come closer to a metal object, there is a moment when the metal object jumps at speed towards the magnet. Science seems to have found a way of harnessing this energy and converting it into electricity, and this electricity will be free. This new knowledge seems to be able for the first time to explain how crystals and gems are able to interact with humans. It's a major breakthrough.

The Law of Belief.

When you begin to use the 'magic' power of your subconscious, then you'll notice small miracles happening around you, and more will come. What do you believe? Because maybe it's not the thing believed in, but the belief itself that brings the results. The law of belief works in all the religions around the world. Buddhist, Hindu, Christian, Moslem and Hebrew all may get some answers through their prayers. Not because of a particular creed, ritual or ceremony, but through belief. The law of life is the law of belief, and belief could be summed up briefly as a thought in the mind.

As a man thinks, feels and believes, so is the condition of his mind, body and circumstances. A technique or methodology based on an understanding of what you are doing and why you are doing it will help you to bring about a successful result, a realisation of your heart's desire.

The great secret possessed by the great men of all ages was their ability to contact and release the powers of their subconscious mind.

Visualisation

The easiest and most obvious way to formulate an idea is to visualise it, imagine it in your 'mind's eye', and see it as if it's real. You can see through your eyes what already exists in the outer world, and in a similar way, that which you can imagine and visualise in your mind's eye exists in the invisible realms of the mind. The idea, the thought in the form of your imagination is the substance of things hoped for and the evidence of things to come. The Chinese say, 'A picture is worth a thousand words'. William James, the father of American psychology, stressed the fact that the subconscious mind will bring about any picture held in the mind and backed by feeling and a belief.

Use your Imagination, and not willpower.

When using your subconscious mind you are able to imagine without the interference of any opponent - mainly the intellect, which can be your worst enemy, especially if it decides to be negative. Neither can you use willpower. You will find your intellect trying to get in the way, but persist in maintaining a simple, childlike, miracle-making faith.

The Bible says, 'Therefore I tell you, whatever you ask for in prayer, believe that you have received it, and it will be yours'. How do you believe you have received something? You imagine you already have it. But here is the secret, here is the code: you have to do it with a feeling or with an emotion. For example, if you want to become pregnant then make sure you have a fertility stone like a moonstone; it helps to focus the mind. Now imagine the desired effect, for example a doctor saying, 'Congratulations, you're expecting,' but imagine at the same time how would you feel if that happened. Energise the thought you are bringing from the future into the present, and when you can, the whole of universal law will be at your disposal.

More examples.

You're ill and worried. Get a healing stone (a rose quartz is quite good), quieten the mind, then visualise a friend or someone in the family saying, "You're looking well," and you replying, "I feel great." Even if you feel terrible, that doesn't matter - remember the placebo effect. It's based on a lie. Or, have you got a bad memory? If you have, you can improve it tenfold by not admitting it and in fact by going the other way and repeating, 'I have a good memory, my memory's brilliant, I have total recall.' The fact that you may not is immaterial. The subconscious believes whatever you tell it; this is what a hypnotist relies on. If you want a new job and you have an interview - then get a stone for good luck, or if you're feeling anxious a stone to relax with. Quieten the mind, relax, then imagine it's now after the interview, someone is asking you how it went, and you say something like, "You won't believe this but I got the job!" Then imagine at the same time how would you feel if you had. Get excited, punch the air, remember you've just got the job.

It's imagining a feeling that most people have trouble with. For example, imagine you got into a taxi and gave half a dozen different directions to the driver in the first few minutes of the journey. He would become hopelessly confused and probably would refuse to go anywhere. It's the same when working with your subconscious mind. There must be a clear-cut image in your mind - your visualisation - and it must have the one ingredient that is necessary for universal law to become activated: a feeling, an emotion. Given half a chance, who wouldn't want to be a millionaire? But would you know how it feels to be a millionaire? Get into the part, imagine how it would feel; the rewards are staggering.

An inner child workshop.

In July 1991 I attended a five-day 'inner child' workshop at a retreat in Surrey. It was organised by the 'Sisters of the Cenacle', an international congregation ministering to both men and women of all faiths. The name Cenacle refers to the room where the last supper was celebrated and the Holy Spirit descended onto the apostles. The event was advertised as a workshop to explore the connections between childhood woundedness and areas of adult life. It was run by two sisters, one I believe was well known to the Queen Mum and the other had been to universities in America as part of her studies within the church. They were both very knowledgeable. I thought they were like the Jesuit priests.

At the time I was studying to become a hypnotherapist and thought that this workshop could help me to understand some of my studies. These types of courses are never to be taken lightly, but imagine my surprise when I received a letter, telling me that I had been accepted but going on to say, *'I should like to point out that if you do not have a follow-up support system for yourself, e.g. a counsellor or spiritual director, then the two sisters running the course are not able to accept responsibility for anything which may be surfaced during the workshop. Nor, given the demanding and intense nature of the workshop, will they be able to give extra time for support during it.*

'I would urge you, therefore, to reflect carefully as to whether you still wish to attend the workshop.'

Wow! What a build-up - and I wasn't disappointed. Here is the point of the story: about thirty-five of us had been meditating for nearly two days and I felt it just wasn't touching me; I was expecting more. (I did get more, but not until later on in the week.) I caught one of the sisters and told her how I felt, and she said, "It's because you are already there, Robert. You and three others, you are already where all the others are wanting to be." She went on to say something quite astounding: "You can achieve more in a three-minute prayer than most can in hours." Well, did that give me something to think about! It turned out to be this technique of visualising and imaging with feeling.

The principal reasons for failure are lack of confidence and too much effort. Many people block answers to their prayers by failing to fully understand the workings of the mind. When you know how your mind works, you become more confident. When you imagine the reality of the fulfilled desire and can feel the thrill of its accomplishment, your subconscious mind is activated to bring about the realisation of your dreams, your goals, your desire.

Psalm 19:14.

Maybe this is what the Psalmist really meant when he wrote: **'May the words of my mouth** (our thoughts, mental images and the good) **and the meditations of my heart** (our nature, our feelings and emotions) **be pleasing in thy sight, O Lord** (the law of right thinking of the subconscious mind) **my rock, and my redeemer** (it's the power and wisdom of our subconscious mind that can redeem us from sickness, poverty and misery).

Within each of us is a kind of personalised instruction book revealing where we have come from, where we are going and who we really are. Somehow, in each human there is, deep within the psyche, a knowledge of everything connecting with the universe. It's as if there's a veil that conceals it all. Just as the sun is always shining behind the clouds, waiting to break through, so universal life force waits for our psychological clouds to part. Maybe no one book, prophet or religion possesses the whole and absolute truth, but a value can be found in each and all of them.

What we can choose, especially as we increase in wisdom and years, is the way we approach the circumstances of our lives. Don't we all believe that what we see around us when we walk down the street is an accurate reflection of what really is? What we don't realise is the innumerable forms of energy surrounding us at any given moment. These range from radio signals and light waves to radiation, electricity and magnetism - not to mention our own inner electrical and chemical discharges, our thoughts, senses, feelings and emotions, and so it goes on and on. Discover how to use all this energy by harnessing it; it's all around us.

To summarise: -

From just two common elements, the king and queen of the mineral world, comes Quartz Crystal, a crystal befitting any crown jewels. However, the most amazing and powerful crystal of them all is **MAN**. Where can we find the power to change our lives? It's in the 'Law of Right Thinking'; it's found in the mind.

There are two main parts to the mind, the conscious and the subconscious, and both must be in harmony. Where is the power, then? It's in the mind. Where in the mind? In the subconscious; you can see it at work with the picture of the staircase. But where is it in the subconscious? It's in the Imagination. So how can I activate this power? You must imagine your desired effect or goal; your dream. See them in your mind's eye. Then imagine how would you feel if you achieved it. Energise the thought by adding a feeling. It's called, by some, a 'scientific prayer'. The role of the crystal could be similar to that of a booster station, to help increase the power and relay the message. Just like the mobile phone masts you can see everywhere; they are there to boost the signals.

And finally ...

... on a personal note: In 1986 I sent away for a booklet entitled 'Power for Living'. A package arrived; I opened it, and it wasn't what I expected. However, I did get chance to read it and I found it to be interesting. It was religious and I wasn't. It concluded with a prayer, and I repeated it and signed it to acknowledge that I had read it. Next came a kaleidoscope of emotions and feelings, experiences lasting over an 18-month period. I listened, I studied and I observed. I now write books and give talks on the subject of the mysteries surrounding Gemstones and Crystals.

I have found that the very understanding I discovered in church can also be found outside church. It's in all religions - Christianity, Islam, Judaism, Hinduism, Buddhism etc, even in atheism and agnosticism - and in all walks of life. A tiny minority have said I can't be a Christian because of my views. How nice then, to see the new Archbishop of Canterbury, Dr. Rowan Williams, being admitted to the highest order of Druids; to see the Queen, the head of the Church of England, going into a Moslem mosque and a Hindu and Sikh temple during her Golden Jubilee year. When people ask, I reply that I am a follower of Jesus Christ and his teachings; and if that makes me a Christian then that's what I am. Read what Jesus said about people who think differently:

"Master," said John, "we saw a man driving out demons in your name and we tried to stop him because he is not one of us." "Do not stop him," Jesus said, "for whoever is not against you is for you.". Luke 9 - 49.

Very early on in my search, I was given a 'mission'. I didn't understand it at the time, but it was this: "De-mystify the mysteries". This thought over the years has become all-consuming. These writings are part of that mission. Life is a journey. Live the journey; discover your way, because, for you, your way is the right way.

Whatever has happened in your life up until now, whatever you may have dreamed of, believed in or hoped for, remember it's all now in the past and can't be changed, however hard you wish it could. A new life, a new chance and a new hope now awaits you. But you yourself must take the first step and do the reaching. What was it that Spock used to say? - "Live long and prosper". I couldn't agree more.

Rosewood
P.O. Box 219, Huddersfield, West Yorkshire. HD2 2YT
E-mail enquiries to: info@rosewood-gifts.co.uk

Or why not visit our website for more information:
www. rosewood-gifts.co.uk

Other titles in the 'POWER FOR LIFE' series:

Discover your own Special Birthstone and the renowned Healing Powers of Crystals REF. (BK1) A look at Birthstones, personality traits and characteristics associated with each Sign of the Zodiac – plus a guide to the author's own unique range of Power Gems.

A Special Glossary of Healing Stones plus Birthstones REF. (BK2) An introduction to Crystal Healing, with an invaluable Glossary listing common ailments and suggesting combinations of Gemstones/Crystals.

Create a Wish Kit using a Candle, a Crystal and the Imagination of Your Mind REF. (BK3) 'The key to happiness is having dreams; the key to success is making dreams come true.' This book will help you achieve.

Gemstone & Crystal Elixirs – Potions for Love, Health, Wealth, Energy and Success REF. (BK4) An ancient form of 'magic', invoking super-natural powers. You won't believe the power you can get from a drink!

Crystal Pendulum for Dowsing REF. (BK5) An ancient knowledge for unlocking your Psychic Power, to seek out information not easily available by any other means. Contains easy-to-follow instructions.

Crystal Healing – Fact or Fiction? Real or Imaginary? REF. (BK6) Find the answer in this book. Discover a hidden code used by Jesus Christ for healing, and read about the science of light and colour. It's really amazing.

How to Activate the Hidden Power in Gemstones and Crystals REF. (BK7) The key is to energise the thought using a crystal. The conscious can direct – but discover the real power. It's all in this book.

Astrology: The Secret Code REF. (BK8) In church it's called 'Myers Briggs typology'. In this book it's called 'psychological profiling'. If you read your horoscope, you need to read this to find your true birthstone.

Talismans, Charms and Amulets REF. (BK9) Making possible the powerful transformations which we would not normally feel empowered to do without a little extra help. Learn how to make a lucky talisman.

A Guide to the Mysteries surrounding Gemstones & Crystals REF. (BK10) Crystal healing, birthstones, crystal gazing, lucky talismans, elixirs, crystal dowsing, astrology, rune stones, amulets and rituals.

A Simple Guide to Gemstone & Crystal Power – a mystical A-Z of stones REF. (BK11) From Agate to Zircon, all you ever needed or wanted to know about the mystical powers of gemstones and crystals.

All the above books are available from your local stockist,
or, if not, from the publisher.

NOTES

Welcome to the world of Rosewood

An extract from a 'thank- you' letter for one of my books.

"I realised just how much you really had indeed understood me and my need for direction and truly have allowed me the confidence and strength to know and believe I can achieve whatever I want in life"

If you like natural products, hand-crafted gifts including Gemstone jewellery, objects of natural beauty – the finest examples from Mother Nature, tinged with an air of Mystery – then we will not disappoint you. For those who can enjoy that feeling of connection with the esoteric nature of Gemstones and Crystals, then our 'Power for Life – Power Bracelets could be ideal for you. Each bracelet comes with its own guide explaining a way of thinking that's so powerful it will change your life and the information comes straight from the Bible. e.g. read Mark 11: 22

We regularly give inspirational talks on Crystal Power – fact or fiction? A captivating story about the world's fascination with natural gemstones and crystals and how the Placebo effect explains the healing power of gemstones and crystals – it's intriguing. And it's available on a CD

To see our full range of books, jewellery and gifts including CD's and DVD'S

Visit our web site - www.rosewood-gifts.co.uk

To see our latest videos go to 'You Tube' and type in Rosewood Gifts.